AL

A Mother's Guide to Strength, Organization, and Beautiful
Living with an ADHD Child

by Emma Adams

A Free Gift

I would like to say Thank You for buying my book so I put together a free gift for you!

This article is the perfect companion for this book. Please claim your free gift by e-mailing garbte@gmail.com with subject title, "ADHD" and I'll revert back to you with your free gift! :)

Table of Contents

About this Book

Whether you're about to embark on the ADHD journey with your little one, or are in the midst of it, you've come to the right place for some direction and support. Parenting a child with ADHD is no easy task. Whether you're a working, stay-at-home, married or single mom, the added complication of learning new parenting skills and dealing with frustrations is bound to cause strain in many aspects of your life.

As your best-laid plans and great intentions fly out the window, this book aims to support you through the process. It whittles away at the tomes of information out there. By all means, educate yourself about the condition as far as possible. But when you're feeling overwhelmed and inundated with academic information from the professionals and with advice from well-meaning friends and relatives – this handy little book will hopefully provide you with some answers and a reassuring shoulder to lean on.

It documents the often tumultuous journey of raising a child with ADHD and covers diagnosis, medication, schooling and everything in-between.

Preface

Drawing on my personal experiences only, this book gives as intimate account of a 16-year journey through the highs and lows of raising a child with ADHD. It does not attempt to replace or provide any definitive answers to medical questions. Nor does it aim to influence any treatment plan you may be considering or have decided on.

What it does do is:

-address the issues of anxiety and guilt you may experience as a mother

-give you pause for thought when considering your plan of action to deal with ADHD

-give you both sides of the story that you may not necessarily hear from the professionals

-document failed treatments and poor decisions and lessons learnt the hard way

-sound some warning bells and pointers you may overlook

-provide practical tips and tools that helped us.

And finally, I hope this book will reassure you that you are not alone out there on this often lonely road, that it will restore hope if it's been lost, and that it encourages you to keep celebrating the special child you have been blessed with.

Chapter 1: Are You Sure??? Diagnosis, Dithering and Denial

Chances are that if you're reading this book you've already received a positive Attention Deficit Hyperactivity Disorder (ADHD) diagnosis for your child. If not, and you are plagued with suspicion that your child may suffer from ADHD, I do hope that this account will give you heart. I am mother to both an ADHD and a non-ADHD child. I am also wife to a successful entrepreneur. A situation which saw me as the primary caregiver and which left a lot of the parenting up to me. I once had a successful corporate career of my own and battled to juggle it all. These are my experiences.

Most commonly diagnosed at the age of about 6 years old at the start of schooling, ADHD raises its head most glaringly in the school classroom. Suddenly, the playful hyperactivity, the exuberance and chattiness, the impulsive outspokenness of the first six years of your little one's life are being brought into question. And more than likely, the person to set the alarm bells ringing will be the Grade 1 teacher you had such high hopes of impressing! Or you may have had raised eyebrows from other parents in the supermarket while your little one threw the dreaded tantrum in the sweets aisle. Or a sudden lack of invitations to play dates and parties may have left you feeling confused, snubbed and a little bit hurt. Or perhaps there may have been subtle criticisms from older members of your own family... mutterings of *in my day a hard smack would have sorted that out*.... The opportunities for public censure of an ADHD child are never-ending.

The ADHD child is characteristically loud, overly-energetic, too talkative, and wildly impulsive and thus accident-prone -- all traits that demand attention and are not always socially acceptable. Unfortunately, it's often attention of the wrong kind and you may find, as I did, that you start to avoid outings as they just become too stressful.

My first experience of this criticism and my reaction to it was 'but he's a boy, its normal for them to be playful and fidgety at this age!'. On the day I was called into school, I found myself in the waiting area with four other young moms. We were all being called in for the same reason. Our kids were 'disruptive, talkative, unable to focus and generally being a menace in the classroom'. At the first suggestion of ADHD, I refused to accept the possibility and was horrified at the teacher alluding to medicating my child. *'A very handy way to shut your kids up'* was my first thought. We had no history of this in my family. I was a generally reserved, bookish child growing up. (Although, there was an uncle who was apparently 'very naughty' and did not last long in the schooling system. He landed up travelling the world and later became dependent on alcohol.) My husband was raised in an autocratic, *if you spare the rod; you spoil the child* kind of environment. Any behavioral disorders would have gone undiagnosed on his side of the family. I simply could not understand why this teacher was not seeing the bubbly, charming, funny and creative child I did.

The diagnosis was inescapable though. After I was called in by my son's karate teacher I was forced to admit that something may indeed be amiss. I'm ashamed to say I paid attention this time because the teacher was a toughened male, who I thought would surely be able to handle any high jinx from a seven-year-old boy.

An ADHD diagnosis may only be made by a registered healthcare professional. Several steps are involved in this process and the diagnosis is made by using the *Diagnostic and Statistical Manual of Mental Disorders*, published by the American Psychiatric Association. Only after three consultations with three different independent practitioners was I convinced. My son checked all the boxes (and then some):

Inattentive presentation:

-Fails to give close attention to details or makes careless mistakes

-Has difficulty in sustaining attention

-Does not appear to listen

-Struggles to follow through instructions

-Has difficulty with organization

-Avoids or dislikes tasks requiring a lot of thinking

-Loses things

-Is easily distracted

-Is forgetful in daily activities

Hyperactive-impulsive presentation:

-Fidgets with hands or feet or squirms in chair

-Has difficulty remaining seated

-Runs about or climbs excessively

-Difficulty engaging in activities quietly

-Acts as if driven by a motor

-Talks excessively

-Blurts out answers before questions have been completed

-Difficulty waiting or taking turns

-Interrupts or intrudes upon others

Combined inattentive and hyperactive-impulsive presentation:

-Has symptoms from both of the above presentations

http://www.adhdawarenessmonth.org/symptoms-and-diagnosis/

Reference: American Psychiatric Association (2013). Diagnostic and Statistical Manual of Mental Disorders (DSM-5), Washington, D.C.: American Psychiatric Association.

It was as if the checklists had been written exclusively for him. The tests and checklists were exhaustive and done in consultation with his teacher. They were completed over a period of six months and the findings were consistent. Yes, his behavior was impacting his life negatively. I was forced to concede this watching him struggle to complete his homework. Watching him being shunned by friends in the park when he butted in and could not wait his turn to go on the swings. His moods swung from exuberance at being allowed to play in the park to anger as his play date ended in shambles. He was constantly frustrated as he battled to understand the consequences of his behavior.

In hindsight, I should have taken him for testing earlier. My stubbornness and denial had prolonged his misery and I felt anxious about the future and guilt at my lack of parenting skills. I was saddened by the prospect that he would be facing so many challenges in life and my overwhelming instinct was to protect him, put a band aid on it, and make it all better. I was determined to tackle this 'problem' much as I would any other in any area of my life. With a clear plan of action and clinical no-nonsense approach. My feelings of guilt were compounded by one psychiatrist who said to me 'depriving your child of medication is like depriving a diabetic of insulin'. The guilt and pressure was overwhelming and counter-productive. I found a support group for parents and found their guidance in the coming months invaluable.

Tellingly, of the four children in his Grade 1 class who came in for that dreaded meeting, only one other was diagnosed with ADHD. I still believe that ADHD is being over diagnosed and has become a quick fix label for kids.

Do yourself a favor if you suspect that your child suffers from ADHD:

-Speak to the teacher – if you haven't already been summoned to school!

-Find three reputable, registered healthcare professionals and make an appointment to see them as soon as possible. Have three independent tests done and trust your instincts.

-Do not Google and attempt to self-diagnose. The information available online is overwhelming.

And if the diagnosis is indeed positive, don't beat yourself up about it. It is a clinical and manageable condition. It in no way diminishes your parenting skills and nor does it make your child abnormal. Your child can be successful and happy, it may just not fit in with the 'white picket fences' picture you had envisioned before. Once you are armed with this knowledge you'll be able to act positively to help your child instead of acting from a place of fear and anxiety. What follows in chapters to come is my path to acceptance and dealing with this disorder.

Chapter 2: What Now...? Looking Back and Looking Forward

Arriving at the stage of acceptance was not an easy path for me. Riddled with self-doubt and *what ifs*, I questioned everything I had done in the preceding six years. Although I was assured that the condition was clinical and as such manageable, I still kept wondering if there was anything I could have done to avoid it. Had I been too lenient with his baby routine? Should I have breastfed for longer? Would the organic, preservative-free baby foods have been better for him? More puzzles and less cartoons? More rules and more structure??

Some therapy and many support group meetings later I was able to put these issues to rest and accept that ADHD is a purely clinical condition. Absolutely nothing you do as a parent during the early years will mitigate any of the symptoms.

After much research and confused by an overwhelming amount of information, I realized that I could not do this on my own. I needed to educate those around me, starting with members of my own family. The psychologist we settled on prescribed a team approach with close and regular co-operation and communication between

-us all as a family
-the teachers at school
-the therapists and anyone my son came into contact with during his sporting and extra-curricular activities.

I felt a profound sense of relief at this. Accepting that my son had ADHD required a huge re-adjustment of my own mindset. I needed to understand his challenges and limitations and to change my own expectations. Simple parenting strategies which had so far largely failed needed to be abandoned. And from within I needed to find the strength to be consistent, the patience to constantly work at these new challenges with him and the faith to believe that all would indeed be fine.

As any working mother out there, I too led a life of balancing the many roles I needed to play. It was a challenge to stop myself from overcompensating for this child who needed me to be to be his strongest supporter. I constantly needed to keep myself in check. Was this misdemeanor 'naughtiness' or because of ADHD? Do I excuse this behavior and explain to the offending parties or do I punish? Would people think that I am being over-protective of him and making excuses? I think that for many parents out there this is something we frequently battle with. And frequently this is also the source of much marital tension. Very often, mom is a lot more forgiving than dad… and a lot more prone to protect and justify the offending behavior.

> -Research as much as possible… try to understand
> the condition and see the world through your child's
> eyes
> -Find a support group in your area -- a friendly chat
> over a cup of tea can do wonders when you're
> feeling exhausted, emotionally wrung out or in
> doubt
> -Let go of your 'white picket fence' expectations –
> they are simply not going to happen

In the next chapter, you'll get a glimpse of the multi-disciplinary approach to treating and managing ADHD.

Chapter 3: Getting a Handle on It: A Plan of Action

Our psychologist recommended a multi-disciplinary approach, which was to include:

-Medication – Ritalin
-Natural supplements
-A change in diet
-Behavioral therapy

Feeling hopeful and determined, I embraced the new regime with enthusiasm. At this stage I had become quite desperate. My son had been having ongoing problems in the classroom, and was becoming unhappy and rebellious. By nature, sunny and outgoing his personality was being perceived as being brash and attention-seeking. Constant punishment at school was having the opposite effect. The more attention he received for his negative behavior, the more he behaved in this way. His impulsivity prohibited him from keeping himself in check. All I wanted was for him to be OK and happy – and not endanger anyone else in the process!

The first and most dramatic step we took was looking at the possibility of medication…

Chapter 4: Medication

At the first mention of medication I was skeptical and fearful. I had always favored a more natural approach to managing our family's health. I researched and found every single piece of information I could about Ritalin, the most commonly prescribed stimulant drug used to treat ADHD.

Our doctor spoke about it as if it was the Holy Grail of medications. His teacher looked quite delighted when I mentioned that I was considering it as a treatment. Members of the parents support group were split. Some swore by it and said that it had 'saved' their child. Others said it was a no-no.

Ritalin is well-documented as being controversial. The literature warned of side-effects such as insomnia, loss of appetite, abdominal cramps, the development of facial tics and an increased heart rate and chest pains amongst many others. Our doctor assured us that these side-effects were not severe, would wear off after the first few months and would not necessarily present in everyone. In fact, they were negligible when compared to the gains offered by the medication. I had read up on so many success stories of children being treated with Ritalin. Their focus in the classroom had improved, their self-esteem was bolstered and they were happy and doing well.

I warily started my son on a very low dose of Ritalin when he was 7 years old. On the first day, I kept him home from school as I wanted to monitor the effects of the medication myself. (In fact, I was so hesitant about my decision, that I took Ritalin myself on the first day and I did not give it to him! Incidentally, I felt no effect.) After four days at home and administering a very low dosage, he seemed to be fine. Slightly more subdued and more attentive than he usually was. This seemed to bode well and I felt more at ease about my decision.

I happily packed my son off to school with his new medication and a note for the teacher to administer half the dosage at during recess. I had high hopes and felt confident about the future.

Two weeks later, his teacher sent a glowing report about his improved concentration, handwriting and general behavior. I was relieved and thrilled that we had found such an easy remedy. At the back of my mind I still suffered from nagging worries about the side-effects. His healthy appetite had all but disappeared. He had started to lose some weight and while I tried to justify it as him growing out of his puppy fat, I was uneasy. He slept restlessly and had blue circles under his eyes. Our doctor assured us that these side- effects would pass.

The doctor adjusted his medication and prescribed a slow-release version of Ritalin. This meant that the effects of the medication would not peak but would be slowly released into his system all day. I was told that his appetite should improve and that soon he would start to sleep more soundly. Still the raving school reports continued to pour in. But I had noticed a change in my child's personality. Gone were the daily jokes and wit and sparkle which had made him so special. Accustomed to him bouncing out of bed each morning filled with energy and a zest for life which I found irresistible, he was now slightly sluggish and carried about him an air of heaviness. His heaviness affected my mood. I had not before appreciated how much I depended on his ear-to-ear smile in the morning, how much of his inner joy was infectious. He was a shadow of the lively little boy he had been. Alarmingly, he had also developed a slight twitch in his left eye, which he seemed to have no control over. Every time his eye twitched, my stomach knotted with anxiety.

It broke my heart to see him like this and yet I ploughed on, giving in to pressure from society. He was fitting in at school and with his peers, but he was like a robot -- following instructions quietly. Ritalin had made him amenable and pliable and had robbed him of his personality.

Six months later, he was winded playing a game of rugby after school. I was summoned from my office and rushed him to the local emergency room as he had chest pains. When the attending doctor was told he was on Ritalin, they performed an ECG (Electric Cardiogram to monitor the heart's activity). In sheer terror at the implications, I abandoned the medication immediately. I had had enough and had put him through enough. The health risks were simply not worth it. I was very happy to have my son back after almost ten months of Ritalin treatment.

I have heard many success stories in our support group and many children seemed to have thrived on being treated with Ritalin, Adderall or Concerta. Many parents have told me that they too were alarmed at some of the side-effects but that they had lessened over time, and indeed some children seem to present with no side-effects whatsoever. Sadly, this was not to be in our case. I was chided for being impatient and for not giving my son a fighting chance. I was to question myself on this years later, when my son seemed to battle with lapses in his ADHD management. But I have never been convinced that it was the right thing for him – it certainly wasn't for me as I didn't have the stomach for it.

Whichever route you decide to follow, research the medication and its side-effects carefully. Ask questions of your doctor and speak to other parents who are using the same treatment. Know what to expect. Do not feel pressurized into your decision and do not make your decision out of fear. As a parent you have a right to choose.

And do not discount the possibility of homeopathic treatment… it may just be a viable alternative for you too as the next chapter foes on to explain.

Chapter 5: Natural Supplements

The decision to cease medication was met with horror by my son's teacher and our GP. I was made to feel as if I was doing him a huge disservice. But, bolstered by the strength of my convictions this time around, I decided to take matters into my own hands. I had decided that I would much rather have a child bursting with energy and life than one drugged up and looking at life from the outside in, because despite the challenges he had faced in the past few months he was as resilient and good-natured as ever.

I turned to the services of a registered homeopath who recommended daily doses of:

-Evening primrose oil
-Omega 3
-Zinc

These supplements are all essential for good brain functioning and development. After two months, I noticed a shift for the better in my son's focus and attention span. Rave reports were no longer pouring in from school but nor were excessive complaints. I decided to settle for this happy medium and felt quietly optimistic. This on its own was not enough though, and our family's eating habits came under scrutiny as you're about to discover.

Chapter 6: Diet

At the best of times, it's a challenge to keep ones kids on the straight and narrow when it comes to eating healthily. This difficulty is compounded by the fact that 50% of the day is spent at school and extra-mural activities where other food choices are available to them. Telling a seven-year-old boy to opt for an apple instead of a candy bar is nigh impossible, and so it becomes very hard to implement and maintain a controlled diet. In addition, we're bombarded by all manner of commercially produced foods aimed specifically at our children.

I was forced to (guiltily) review exactly what I was feeding my family. And although it was generally healthy, I did rely on take-away meals on those evenings I worked late. I happily arrived home bearing Happy Meals a bit too often. I did not buy candy, but we loved chocolate and sodas. I allowed sugary cereals simply because it was the only breakfast I could be assured would be eaten. And these doubled up as a dry snack during the day! Friday nights were sugar and carbohydrate feasts and I was a very willing participant. I was quite dismayed at the rut I had allowed us to slip into – it was a far cry from the balanced diet I had been raised on as a child.

An overhaul of our diet was needed, for not just my son's sake but for ours too. I had been running on empty for months, eating for the sake of it. Dietary changes would need commitment from us all as a family. (My husband took to keeping a private stash of crisps in his own closet.)

Foods I eliminated over time (and whose elimination showed positive results) included:

-Added sugar in all its forms, including fruit juices -- which he had an insatiable thirst for

-Tartrazine and other food colorings – which meant all manner of snacks needed to be outlawed

-Caffeine – our home became a soda-free zone

I aimed to keep his blood sugar levels constant and avoided any foods which would spike them. These included white carbohydrates such as:

-white flours (white breads and pastries)

-potatoes

-white rice

I replaced these with wholegrain and low Glycaemic index foods, which would ensure a slow release of sugar into the blood stream. The much-loved, popular breakfast cereals were replaced with yoghurts and muesli or a slice of wholegrain bread with peanut butter. I introduced more protein-rich foods into our meals, as well as omega 3 rich fish at least twice a week as well as copious amounts of vegetables. Some bribery and compromise was needed – if the *Super-veg* broccoli was eaten he could ignore all the other green vegetables. Fortunately, my husband is a dab hand at Asian-style cooking so this did not present too much of a problem for us.

The *no-sugar rule* was met with much resistance and was almost impossible to implement outside of the home. Parties and social gatherings became a nightmare as he was too young to exercise self-control. The *no-sugar rule* was relaxed into a *limited sugar rule*, and I would prepare myself for the worst after he had been to a party. I had to compromise and managed to consistently reinforce a controlled diet during the week when he had to attend school. This, in the end, yielded positive results. Weekends were a hit-and-miss affair and we treated this as his 'down time'.

On the school front, I lobbied for a review of the school canteen's offering. This was supported by many other parents, and slowly healthier options were introduced. The school tuck shop no longer served any sweets, sodas or crisps during first and second recess but only after school. At the end of the first year, teachers reported a dramatic improvement in classroom focus and attentiveness as a whole.

-Phase out the sugar in stages – to eliminate it suddenly will be met with resistance
-If elimination is not possible, compromise and eliminate it during the school-going week
-Start introducing alternatives to sugary snacks and phase their introduction into the cookie jar– nuts, dried fruit, popcorn
-Review your child's daily food intake – you'd be surprised at the levels of hidden sugars hidden in our most popular snacks
-Pack a lunch box as it gives you some measure of control during the day
-Consider replacing refined white carbohydrates with wholegrain alternatives – bread, rice and crackers can be replaced without too much of a fuss
-Omega 3s found in oily fish is critical for optimal brain development and functioning – aim to make it part of your weekly meal plan
-Avoid processed foods – they are of very little nutritional value and are loaded with artificial colorants
-Changes in diet need to be committed to by the entire family – you cannot continue to keep a candy jar in sight and expect your child not to be tempted.

Balancing the demands of modern day living is no easy feat, and even more so for the mother of an ADHD child. Think of incorporating the changes to your family's diet as a way of improving your entire family's health for the better and for the long-term. These changes are all sustainable and 15 years later, we still adhere to many of them. Like all modern, growing families we do indulge – but it is now in moderation and with mindfulness we did not have before. I found it useful to plan the week's meals in advance. It simplified my life, made shopping and cooking easier and lessened the chances of 'picking something up' on the way home from work. Eating out has never been problematic and it's something we enjoy doing as a family – the only difference now is that we make healthier choices and avoid certain restaurants like the plague.

Interestingly as my son has gotten older, he has become an extremely healthy eater. He has adopted a fairly restrictive diet which I sometimes balk at. But, he has chosen to continue this route in managing his ADHD and has taken responsibility and ownership of it. I sometimes worry that he has become obsessive about it (and his exercise routine), but when I consider the alternatives, I breathe a sigh of relief. He occasionally has a sugar binge, which he indulges in consciously. It's become a family joke and he'll sometimes warn us to 'stand back and watch the fireworks'. I'm proud of the sense of responsibility and mindfulness he has developed.

My son's irrepressible good humor has carried us through so many dark moments during these years. Although he is the one afflicted with this disorder and the one who has to battle through daily challenges, he has always, always managed to turn the situation around and have us in stitches in no time. On a good day (or sometimes a good hour), you could not ask to be in the company of a more kind-hearted, generous and loving soul.

The above interventions were nothing compared to what we learnt through therapy sessions though. What follows is an honest account of our experiences.

Chapter 7: Therapy

The psychologist suggested therapy to deal with issues of:
  -parenting strategies and skills which needed to be learnt
  -behavior modification therapy for my son to equip him with skills to deal with challenging situations
  -relationship therapy for my husband and I to manage the tensions in our home which resulted from our sometimes differing viewpoints

Weekly sessions of behavior modification therapy were suggested for both my son and I. My husband attended a few of these sessions and they helped to give him some insight into managing our day-to-day life at home. At this stage our family situation had changed and I now had a two-year old daughter to care for as well. My husband's business had really started to take off and I made the decision to start working half-days while exploring the option of becoming an independent contractor. I had had enough of the guilt and anxiety about being an absent mother and I could no longer juggle all my responsibilities successfully. Something had to give.

After two false starts, we finally found a therapist who was a good fit for us. These sessions were extremely useful and practical. I had to learn how to parent this special child of mine and had to let go of unrealistic expectations. I needed to learn to embrace and celebrate his good qualities while managing the traits which made his behavior socially unacceptable and destructive.

I gave up my dreams of him following a career in education or one of the sciences (a family tradition), and began to see him through new eyes. A whole new world of possibilities opened up and I abandoned (with some difficulty), my notions of a 'good education, professional and stable career' which had been fed to me all my life. He would always probably struggle with spelling and he hated reading (except for a spell of *Harry Potter* books, for which I was forever grateful to the author. He re-read the entire series, year after year until he was about 16). At times I could not believe that this was my child. I was super-organized, project managed multiple tasks simultaneously and was generally efficient.

On the other hand, he loved people – he could meet, chat to and charm a group of relative strangers within minutes of meeting them, other parents (to my great confusion!) loved him and would often refer to him as the most polite and respectful child they had ever met. He had the gift of the gab and attracted friends of every sort -- everyone seemed to know him. He was unfailingly generous and big-hearted and would go to great lengths to help anyone in need – very often impulsively so, and he would come home from school starving after handing his lunch over to someone else. He was also a huge champion of the underdog and would (sometimes dangerously impulsively) jump to someone's defense if he thought they needed it. I loved all this about him and it very often made me reflect on my own lack of social skills.

The therapy started off with an initial assessment of our situation. We identified behaviors which were the most damaging and destructive. The therapist then set goals and outcomes and we aimed to address each one individually. This would be done by learning new skills to deal with the problem situation. With the successful attainment of each new 'mini-skill' I was to reward the behavior. It was critical to apply this consistently in both the home and school environment.

It also included practical advice on strategies on managing the home and school situation.

An example of a problem identified which was impacting my son's daily life negatively, was chronically bad time management. This spilled over into every aspect of his life from school to sport to social commitments. On the home front, it was a constant bugbear. Although our daily lives were largely regulated, we would occasionally make a spontaneous decision to visit a restaurant on a week evening. My husband felt strongly that we could not allow ADHD to take over all our lives. Much frustration and irritation would ensue when we were all kept waiting in the car for 30 minutes because he could not find his shoe / or decide what to wear. Very often the rest of the evening would be dismal and overshadowed by simmering irritation. The therapist advised us to handle those situations in the following way:

> -At least 40 minutes before leaving the house, issue a clear, simple instruction to be ready within 30 minutes and promise a reward if he manages to be on time
>
> -Break the instruction down into *please go and choose an outfit to wear / please comb your hair / please check your pockets and make sure you have your phone, iPod, etc.*
>
> -After 30 minutes check on progress and encourage if necessary
>
> -If he manages to be ready on time, even if he only just manages it, praise his efforts. Point out that you appreciate his efforts and that everyone can now look forward to the evening ahead.

We were to apply these principles in every situation that needed time management and over time, with consistent reinforcement he was able to manage these situations without too much micro-management from me.

Another example, was attempting to temper his (sometimes) over-confidence and thinking without speaking in social situations. Very often, these had the potential to cause offence when none was intended. His impulsivity led to him not being able to filter his thoughts and sometimes make cringe-worthy, inappropriate comments. This was a particularly difficult one to deal with and over many sessions, the therapist dealt with it by:

-discussing and identifying comments which he had found to be hurtful in the past
-role-playing these situations with him
-in a group session, asking me to recall comments he had made which had caused offence to people
-role-playing these situations with him being on the receiving end of these comments
-asking him to identify the hurt these comments now caused him
-slowly waking him up to the realization that flippant comments caused harm and showing him how they affected others' perception of him (this was a particular breakthrough, as he had an overwhelming need to be liked and accepted)

On a practical management level I had to:
-at the first mention of an inappropriate comment to me, calmly raise my hand as if in a STOP sign
-without reacting to the comment, calmly say... *just think of how you would feel if I said that to you...*
-wait for his response – which would invariably be *... not nice I suppose...*
-Follow up with... *would you like to repeat that in a nicer way... or would you like to take those words back...?*
-A positive response from him would be followed up with... *don't you feel better that you have not hurt my feelings..?*
-A defiant response of... *I don't care...* would result in a follow up of... *this conversation is over*, a silent treatment and no further responses from me and as much as it pained me I would have to walk away

27

This intervention was particularly frustrating and draining. It was later expanded on to include pausing before speaking and considering the other person's feelings. In social situations, I would pointedly look at him and raise my hand slightly when I anticipated a 'problem' situation. I had to physically act as the pause button to enable him to stop and consider his next words before uttering them.

Of all the challenges we have faced, I have found it the most difficult to move along with his sudden changes in behavior. He would recover from an angry outburst within a few minutes, whereas I would still be smarting from it. It has also turned out to be the most valuable for me. Through therapy I have had to learn to let go of lingering irritation, impatience and sometimes anger -- and move along with it. It's changed me and I have become more patient, forgiving and understanding.

Pearls of wisdom I've retained...

-Try to differentiate between negative behaviors. Is this related to ADHD? Did he neglect to do a chore because he became distracted? Not punishable... Or did he neglect to do it because he was being defiant? Punishable...

-Praise and reinforce good behavior

-Don't sweat the small stuff. Your ADHD child will probably not be able to maintain a spotlessly clean room all the time. And he probably won't be able to do the dishes without walking off at least once.

-Praise the EFFORT he makes and not the end result

-Plan ahead as far as possible. An ADHD child does not cope well with sudden changes in routine or being made to wait. If you can avoid these situations, avoid them.

In the next chapter, I detail some simple steps to implement at home in the hopes of creating a calmer, more harmonious environment for your family.

Chapter 8: Strategies for a Peaceful Home

8.1 Establish a Routine

When I no longer had to juggle the demands of a full-time job, I found it much easier to implement a fairly rigid daily routine. I've found this to be an essential part of ADHD management. As organization and time management are huge challenges, a routine is invaluable in getting through the day without any upsets, procrastination and confrontations. It quiets the mind and limits choices so that the child is able to transition through the day without any hiccups. Once I had established a:

-homework

-free outside playtime

-dinner

-bath

-bed routine, his response was remarkable.

He seemed to enjoy the boundaries I had set for him and was able to function within those parameters. As he got older, these routines were obviously adjusted but in essence we retained the structure. During his teen years he established his own 'Sunday night' routine, which entailed a complete spring clean of his closets and bedroom, organization of his desk and numerous facial and hair treatments (much to my amusement). He would then be set for the week.

School holidays were a challenge for all of us as there was simply no routine. Fortunately he has always been active and sporty and I would encourage him to go for a jog or a swim every morning. I can't profess to have had much success with the rest of the unregimented time during holiday seasons. In hindsight, these were our most stressful times when in actual fact, they should have been the happiest and most carefree. Holiday trips needed to be carefully considered and planned with military precision. A seven-hour road trip needed to be broken up into manageable chunks, with an activity planned at each pit stop. A once-in-a-lifetime trip to Disneyland very nearly turned into sheer disaster when our shuttle bus abandoned us and I had to resort to Plan B. He simply could not deal with the disappointment, sudden change in plan and the wait. But, true to form, once the tantrum had passed he charmed us all back into holiday spirit and laughter and all was forgiven.

8.2 Limiting Stimuli – The Twenty TV Screens

'Twenty TV screens flashing at once' was how my son once described a trip with me to the shopping mall amid the pre-Christmas shopping frenzy. The crowds of people, lighting and screaming signs in each shop window, the overhead lights, decorations and constant Christmas jingles proved too much for him. It was simply sensory overload. I understood then how he perceived these situations and what a challenge and unnecessary hardship it was for him. After that, I simply left him at home.

I limited TV watching to 30 minutes a day, with the exception of the occasional family show we would watch together. The less stimuli he had thrown at him, the better he was able to focus.

In later years, this included a 'no-cell-phone after 7pm 'rule.

The one thing I did allow freely was music. He'd been passionate about music all his life and from the age of three, needed only to hear a song once or twice to remember all the lyrics. He seemed to be able function better with it and to this day cannot wash the dishes without wearing his earphones. It seems to quiet the white noise around him and he is able to focus on the task at hand to the exclusion of all else. As a young adult now, driving his own car, he often has to turn back home to collect his favorite CD as he simply cannot drive without it.

As with many ADHD children, he was creative and would spend hours at his computer designing graphics. This would hold his attention for hours on end and proved to be a great outlet and channel for his mental energy.

8.3 Clear Communication

Keep instructions clear and simple. I would often get frustrated when my son could not seem to follow the simplest of instructions. I learned that *clean your room* would yield no results. I needed break it down into: *make up your bed*; tidy *up your toys*; *pick up your shoes*. And I needed to give a time limit with it. *Please make your bed in the next 15 minutes*, would get a response.

I also learnt to first get his attention and make eye contact before speaking and when I saw the tell-tale signs of his wandering attention, I would ask him to repeat the instruction to me. All of these little extras can be time-consuming and draining, but once they become a habit are ultimately rewarding and save you both unnecessary frustrations.

8.4 Banishing Clutter and Keeping Organized

The ADHD child creates the very situation he is unable to function within. The bane of the every parent's life -- the untidy bedroom -- reaches new levels with the ADHD child. I would implement regular decluttering sessions, with his co-operation.

Some practical tips I found useful in his personal space:

-I invested in sets of clear plastic box containers for toy storage and easy access. This helped with cleaning up easily and minimized his frustration when looking for something in particular.

-I labeled the shelves in his closet: school clothing, rugby kit, rough and tumble clothing, swimming clothing, etc

-His closets were organized and packed according to outfits'. For example some t-shirts and shorts were packed together, as opposed to stacking all t-shirts together on one shelf and all shorts together on another. Matching shirts and trousers were hung together on one hanger. This enabled him to grab an outfit and get dressed, instead of hauling everything out on to the floor and sifting through them.

-I had a special clothes hanger custom-printed with his name on it. This was the special one to be used each day for his school blazer.

-I installed a hat stand at the door to his room. This was the holder for locker keys, school bag, peak cap, scarf and any other daily essentials – EVERY DAY

Some practical tips I found useful in the family home:

-I extended the weekly timetable to include the entire family, albeit a less detailed version. Dinner times and chores were clearly highlighted. Attendance at family social events were clearly marked up for him to see. It assisted him to know that for example, on Thursday evening at 6pm, we were going to gran's birthday dinner and that his daily schedule would be disrupted.

-I learnt to let go of the small stuff. It was enough that he was at his desk studying. I could not get angry about the trail of study snacks he had dropped making his way to his desk.

-Meal times were kept set at certain times as far as possible and they were communal. TV dinners were never allowed.

-During the earlier years, I used a reward chart to reward chores well attempted (much as they do in school). This was a great incentive.

While the home situation seemed to be under slightly better control, I was at the mercy of a schooling system simply not designed to manage children afflicted with ADHD. This was one area that remained challenging. I hope that our experiences detailed in the next chapter will provide some pause for thought as you consider schooling options for your child.

Chapter 9: Surviving School

School was, simply put, a nightmare. As I had decided to forego conventional medicine and attempt to treat naturally, my relationships with teachers had a rocky start. The ADHD child is understandably a challenging one to deal with in a classroom situation. The natural supplements, dietary changes and behavior modification therapy had shown a measure of success. He was no longer as disorganized and disruptive. His grades had improved. I was no longer hauled in to school regularly to discuss his behavior. Nevertheless, I felt marginalized and felt that he had been labeled as 'the naughty one'.

After a few years, I felt that my son would benefit from a smaller, more one-on-one classroom situation where the staff was equipped to deal with ADHD. This was a huge mistake and set his (and my own) progress back badly. Each child in the classroom was challenged by ADHD. Some were on prescription medication and some were not. They were all affected with different degrees of severity and were at different stages in their treatments and interventions. This environment brought out the worst in his behavior and in a very short space of time he seemed to regress. He no longer had to keep himself in check and consider the consequences of his actions. He saw others act out impulsively and followed suit. I was very glad to see the back of this stage and embrace the challenges of high school.

Although mainstream high school brought its own set of challenges, my son had by then largely recovered from the setbacks of the previous year. Once again forced to comply in a mainstream school environment, he quickly fell into step. I suspect that the onset of puberty had a positive role in this. There was an ample and captive audience for his charm, sense of humor and wit. He was extremely popular and sporty. Although he continued to challenge his teachers, they seemed to be able to manage him and he would often engage them in debate (which they found amusing) as opposed to defying them. His school reports continued to be erratic and would veer from A's in some subjects to barely passing others. There was no pattern to this and all I could attribute it to was how well his ADHD was being managed at that point.

It was with a massive exhalation of relief that I embraced him when he received his final results saying that he had passed with university entrance requirements. The twelve years of schooling were behind us.

Essential practical tips that got us through 12 years of schooling:

At all costs, try to keep lines of communication open with teachers. This is challenging and sometimes embarrassing, but essential

-Make use of a homework diary every day. Ask the teacher to make a note of any requests in it. We all know what it's like to be scrambling around for empty jars or tissue boxes at 6am in the morning.

-Pack a lunch every day and always include some snacks. Blood sugar levels need to remain as stable as possible throughout the day.

-If possible, review what is being sold at the school tuck shop. If you're not happy with it, lobby for change.

-Again, do not feel pressurized into medicating your child – the school has no right to insist on this.

-Attempt to find a school which is a good fit for your child. This is not an easy one, but be wary of the negative labels assigned at school. They are all too real and can become self-fulfilling.

And at home:

-I kept his desk completely clear, save for two pen holders – again nothing to distract him while working. No gadgets to click, no paper clips to twirl and no staples to build a tower out of.

-All blank paper sheets were kept in a drawer and out of site – he loved to draw and would doodle at the slightest opportunity.

-I printed out a weekly timetable on an A3 page and laminated it. I would stick this above his desk. Each day had a column and was printed in a different color. I would include time slots and type some of the information in them. For example, Monday 6.30am: brush teeth… 7pm: have breakfast and vitamins…. 8am: double check school bag and take to car…. Then the later afternoon routine slots I would also fill in, for example, 4pm: Check homework diary and pack homework books onto desk. 4.15pm: Start homework and tick off each completed homework section in diary… 5pm: Call mom to check homework and sign homework diary.

-The weekly timetable would also have blank slots. We would fill these in together during the Sunday evening weekly preparations. These would include breakdowns for projects due, for example, start researching Egypt, Ask mom to buy color board for Egypt, Start making notes for Egypt. We always allowed a day's grace for checking the project. And most importantly, on due date, pack Egypt project into school bag!

-All school worksheets were kept in separate color-coded files and each subject was assigned a different color. We carried this color-coding through to his book covers and anything related to that subject. (To this day, Mathematics will remain blue in my mind!)

-I kept a separate stationery set for his home desk and one for school. He was not allowed to use the contents of his pencil bag a home – they would simply never make their way back to school again!

-All posters and pictures were mounted on a wall he could not see when he was seated at his desk as they once again proved to be a distraction.

-I decided not to sweat the small stuff, and went through millions of lunch boxes and water bottles…

As a result of these enormous challenges, I became incredibly 'tuned in' to my son and his thoughts and behaviors. This was crucial to be able to pre-empt possible awkward situations and allowed me to plan around possibly explosive situations. This bond remains although he is now a young adult. Unfortunately it also became a source of tension in my marriage.

Chapter 10: Marital Strain

I had admittedly devoted a large part of my time and energy to my son's well-being to the exclusion of everything and everyone else. In the period directly after his diagnosis, finding a *cure* for ADHD became something of an obsession for me. Already an avid reader by nature and possessing a can-do, fix-it personality, I cut myself off from everyone else (except my son) and immersed myself in everything I could find on the subject. In addition, I was experiencing my own emotional upheaval. Not surprising then, that my husband felt excluded and resentful. He too, was as concerned and anxious about the diagnosis and about the future. We just had different ways of dealing with it. In the evenings I would regale him with either the day's events at school – positive or negative – the latest information I had found or a new schedule I had devised. My son became the centre of my world which left no space for my husband as a person or for our relationship.

To frustrate the situation even more he and I had had a vastly different upbringing which affected our parenting styles. My parents had been more liberal and indulgent and his were the polar opposite. Although we had, earlier on in our relationship, recognized this and swore not to repeat the mistakes we felt our own parents had made, raising a child with ADHD invariably put a strain on our intentions.

My husband was open and willing to go for therapy to deal with our son's ADHD management and he did. What we did not do timely was to go for therapy ourselves. ADHD had become an all-consuming priority and although my husband actively played his role in its management, he refused to centre our family's life around it. He harbored feelings of jealously about our son's needs taking precedent over his and the general well-being of our family's.

My son picked up on this and sadly played us up against each other. It was a classic good cop/bad cop situation. I would make excuses and over-compensate for him and my husband would accuse him of using ADHD as an excuse and getting away with murder. He did have manipulative tendencies.

It was only much later, after a tumultuous few years that we approached a therapist to deal with our situation. It was then that I was able to acknowledge this. It's imperative that you and your partner seek help at the same time as you do for your child. Divorce rates are sadly closely linked to the prevalence of ADHD in society.

Therapy taught us to:
-go back to the basics and define our own
relationship as partners instead of only as parents
-acknowledge the bond we had and the reasons for
it
-realize that parenting was one aspect of our
relationship and not the be all and end all of it
-communicate our disagreements at the earliest
opportunity and to attempt to resolve them (before
they turned into lingering resentments)
-acknowledge the role each one played in the family
at large and to value this
-present a united front and to be seen to be doing so
(even if we disagreed with each other)
-support each other, especially when we had to
make an unpopular parenting decision
-back each other up with implementing discipline
-recognize the symptoms when the other one has
had enough and to step in to try and defuse the
situation
-allow each other time out on our own to preserve
all-round sanity

-and lastly, to schedule time out together as a couple.

Relationship therapy had come in the nick of time and had forced me to admit that I had allowed my maternal instincts to kick into overdrive dangerously and very closely to everyone's detriment. We pulled back from the edge of a family breakdown and my son responded to this remarkably well. When 'no' from one meant 'no' from us both his boundaries were reinforced.

We were fortunate in that our marriage had not become a casualty of our situation and that therapy had saved us. Unfortunately, the same cannot be said of all relationships with family and friends.

Chapter 11: Family, Friends and Support

Explaining my son's diagnosis to family and friends drew differing responses from both members of our families and our friends. For the most part it was met with empathy and understanding but sometimes it was not. Some who started out being understanding either lost patience, got too irritated or found something about my son's behavior offensive. There were others who seemed to be morbidly fascinated at the challenges we faced and would engage in constant comparisons between their child (who did not suffer from ADHD) and ours. Many relationships fell by the wayside over the years and I did not have the energy or inclination to revive them.

I am blessed and will be eternally grateful to my parents for their unwavering support of our family situation. They seemed to possess an innate sense of when we were experiencing an upheaval. Without too many questions, they would provide a 'second home' for my son. This was his time out and ours too. Weekends at granny's and grandpa's were spent fishing, hiking, dancing and being crazy. They placed no limitations on his behavior and for some reason he did not ever act up with them.

I have a few very good solid friendships too, which provided a safety net for all of us. They 'got' my son, and I was able to socialize freely and comfortably with them with him in tow. They kept him entertained constantly and did not bat an eyelid when he went scooting around their homes knocking vases off tables. They appreciated him for who he was and saw past the chaos he sometimes created. He also made a great playmate for their children, as unlike so many other ADHD sufferers, my son interacted very well with other children of all ages. He was a constant source or rough and tumble for the little ones who would sit on his back while he pretended to be a donkey and would gallop around the house. With the slightly older ones he was a constant source of hilarity as he not only acted as the resident clown but also possessed a sharp and quirky sense of humor way beyond his years.

My son has developed such good relationships with a few of my close friends that he has adopted them as 'surrogate' aunts, and often maintains contact with them independent of my relationship with them.

-Reach out to friends and family
-Surround yourself with support and if you are not used to doing it, start asking for help
-Value these relationships – they'll stand you in good stead in the years to come
-Recognize that some relationships will only function in a child-free zone, and that is okay
-Discard the rest and feel no guilt about it.

Chapter 12: Triggers And Red Flags: How We Survived Them

Formal occasions: notify your child well in advance that you will all be attending a family wedding in two weeks' time. Use the lead up time to the wedding to reinforce the behaviors expected of him at the occasion and break these up into how he should behave during the church ceremony / how he should behave during the family photo session / how he should behave at the reception dinner. Pack in a change of clothing... just in case! Ensure that he has a full meal beforehand, a bottle of water handy and a hand-held (quiet) game to shift his attention to if the formalities become too much. Prepare for the possibility that you may have to leave early. Ironically for such a social character, my son has difficulties coping with large gatherings of people.

Trips to the shopping mall: Avoid them if you can. The sensory overload is sure to set him off. If unavoidable visit the shops during quiet periods and get it over and done with. Dawdling and window-shopping is sure to end in disaster.

Holidays away from home: Plan these with careful consideration. For road trips, discuss the plans with him before the time. Allow him to pack as many toys and activities into his special bag as he wants. Include some snacks for the trip and if possible some earphones and his favorite music. Stop as frequently as you can to alleviate the boredom. For plane trips: Research the destination and attempt to spark his interest and imagination. The anticipation and impatience that can build up during the course of a 12-hour flight can be overwhelming. Pack activity books and attempt to pre-book an aisle seat if possible. My son started experiencing bouts of claustrophobia and frequently needed to get up and walk around.

Large informal family gatherings: We belong to a rather large family and as much as we enjoy getting together I find them trying at times. I would attend only those where an outside play area was easily accessible. For the rest, I would set a time limit of about two hours on it. A period any longer than that would be stressful for him. Again, too many personalities, voices and excitement would result in sensory overload.

This has been a long, hard, challenging and enlightening journey. Each experience along the way has taught us something new. Parenting a child with ADHD has been a blessing in disguise (at times I thought very heavily disguised!). It's taught me to be so much more flexible and open-minded, relaxed and tolerant. I look at him some days and cannot believe that we've made it this far.

Chapter 13: Where we're At Now

I had never before thought to document our experiences of ADHD. Much of it was a blur in my mind until I had started to put pen to paper. I chatted briefly to my son about his recollections of the earlier years. He is horrified at some of the stories and is unwilling to believe he was able to behave in that way. To some extent I believe he has grown out of some ADHD behaviors but I do believe that others have come to take their place. This process has been bittersweet and cathartic.

My son is now a young adult living in a shared flat. He is due to complete his degree in Sport Science in a few months time. His university educational experience passed by relatively smoothly and was helped immeasurably by a multivitamin called Bio-Strath (a Swiss-manufactured product). He has astounded me with his self-motivation. He was able to monitor and regulate himself – seemed to be able to step up to the plate in an environment that did not pose any restrictions on him and his behavior. I am incredibly proud of his achievement.

He still uses large checklists and a massive whiteboard to document his daily tasks. He is slightly obsessive about diet and exercise but this keeps him on the straight and narrow. He is still surrounded by a large network of friends; some have stuck by him since junior school. He drives and maintains his own car – and although he racks up too many traffic fines for my liking – I understand that this is a manifestation of his condition.

I am only allowed to visit him at his flat on Monday mornings and I suspect that this is because he had just done a Sunday night spring clean. He has retained some self-management skills from his childhood. He visits often enough and regularly forgets either his flat keys or mobile phone at our house. I still find myself doing the occasional rescue mission – and my husband still grins and accuses me of mollycoddling him. Our bond is as close as ever, although sometimes we still experience strain in our day-to-day telephone calls when he feels I am checking up on him or being critical.

He recently posted a status on social media saying that he is at his happiest place in his life right now, and that he feels empowered to tackle the future with gusto. He credited my husband and me for getting him there. It drew an overwhelmingly positive response from people, and especially those who knew his journey. (I *liked* it quickly before he got embarrassed about it and *unfriended* me.)

ADHD is a chronic disorder which requires life-long management and never goes away. I am finding it increasingly hard to let go and hand the management of it over to him entirely. I still have feelings of dread and unease when I perceive a threat to his equilibrium on the horizon. I may have to go for another round of therapy, as after all, motherhood is a condition which never goes away…

Did you enjoy this book?

I want to thank you for purchasing and reading this book. I really hope you got a lot out of it.
Don't forget to claim your free gift by e-mailing garbte@gmail.com with subject title, "Free Gift ADHD" and I'll revert back to you with your free gift! :)
.
Can I ask a quick favor though?
If you enjoyed this book, I would really appreciate it if you could leave me a review on Amazon.
I love getting feedback from my readers and reviews on Amazon do make a difference. I read all my reviews and would really appreciate your thoughts.

Thanks so much!
Emma Adams

Made in the USA
Columbia, SC
19 October 2018